THE NATURE COMPANY · YOUNG DISCOVERIES LIBRARY

Incredible
Creatures

Written by Claire Craig

TIME
LIFE
BOOKS

**The Nature Company Young Discoveries Library
is published by Time-Life Books.**

Conceived and produced by
Weldon Owen Pty Limited
43 Victoria Street, McMahons Point,
NSW, 2060, Australia
A member of the
Weldon Owen Group of Companies
Sydney • San Francisco

THE NATURE COMPANY
Priscilla Wrubel, Ed Strobin, Steve Manning,
Georganne Papac, Tracy Fortini

TIME-LIFE BOOKS
Time-Life Books is a division of Time Life Inc.
Time-Life is a trademark of Time Warner Inc. U.S.A.

Vice President and Publisher: Terry Newell
Editorial Director: Donia A. Steele
Director of New Product Development: Regina Hall
Director of Sales: Neil Levin
Director of Financial Operations: J. Brian Birky

WELDON OWEN Pty Limited
President: John Owen
Publisher: Sheena Coupe
Managing Editor: Rosemary McDonald
Project Editor: Libby Frederico
Text Editor: Libby Frederico
Art Director: Sue Burk
Designer: Liz Seymour
Production Manager: Caroline Webber
Vice President, International Sales: Stuart Laurence
Coeditions Director: Derek Barton
Subject Consultants: Daniel Bickel,
Dr. David Kirshner, Terence Lindsey,
Dr. George McKay, Dr. Paul Willis

Library of Congress
Cataloging-in-Publication Data
Incredible creatures / Claire Craig.
   p. cm. -- (Young discoveries)

   ISBN 0-7835-4840-0

   1. Animals--Miscellanea--Juvenile literature.
[1. Animals--Miscellanea.] I. Title. II. Series.
QL49.C696   1996
591--dc20   96-12344

Manufactured by Mandarin Offset
Printed in China

A Weldon Owen Production

Contents

◀ *Scaphognathus* was a flying reptile with very wide wings. It lived at the same time as the dinosaurs.

▼ *Arsinoitherium* was an early mammal with two huge horns, like today's rhinoceroses. It ate grass, leaves, and shrubs.

— I N C R E D I B L E   C R E A T U R E S —

Ancient Creatures

Millions of years ago, the world was very different. As the weather and landscape changed, so did the kinds of creatures that lived on the Earth. Scientists study traces of animal life, such as bones, which have survived through the years. These are called fossils, and they give us clues about when and how animals lived. Some ancient creatures looked like dinosaurs, but lived long before these amazing reptiles. Some looked like animals today. But others were unlike any living creatures.

These animals
are called prehistoric
because they lived
before people
invented writing.

▲ *Dimetrodon* was a
fierce, meat-eating reptile.
It had an enormous fan
perched on its back.

Tusks and Horns

◄ A rhinoceros's horns are made of keratin, which is very hard. They grow back if they are cut off.

◄ Walruses have two tusks. Male walruses fight with their tusks to see which is the strongest.

Some animals have unusual teeth, called tusks. The tooth of the narwhal whale grows until it is about ten feet long. People once thought this ivory tusk had magical powers. Walruses catch food with their tusks. They can also haul their heavy bodies out of the water by hooking their tusks into the ice. Rhinoceroses fight and defend themselves with the horns that grow on their noses.

A unicorn is an imaginary horse with a horn on its head. The narwhal is often called a sea unicorn.

▲ Male narwhals cross their tusks like swords. They fight with each other to mate with females and to be the strongest and most powerful narwhal.

Strange Bills

Many birds have strange bills. A toucan's bright bill is long and looks heavy, but it has pockets of air inside and is very light. Toucans tear off fruit with their bills and reach into nests for eggs. The colored bills of male toucans may attract females. The northern bald ibis wades through water, plucking out fish and frogs with its long, curved bill. The peculiar platypus of Australia is the only mammal with a bill. Because the platypus closes its eyes when it swims underwater, it uses its soft, rubbery bill to feel its way while searching for worms and shellfish to eat.

▲ When a toucan sleeps, it turns its head around and lays its bill down the center of its back.

How does a platypus find food with its eyes closed?

▶ Northern bald ibises nest high in cliffs in Africa. They have no hair on their heads, and look like vultures—birds of prey that feed on dead animals.

◀ The platypus is an unusual mix. It has a duck's bill, an otter's body, and a beaver's tail.

Noses and Tongues

◄ European moles seek out earthworms, beetles, and slugs with their noses and whiskers.

◄ The aardvark's big ears and long nose help it to hear and smell prey.

◄ Desmans are moles that live in the water. They probe beneath rocks with their snouts, looking for insects.

Some creatures have peculiar noses and tongues. The shape of an animal's nose and tongue tells us about the kind of food it eats and where the animal finds it. Short-nosed echidnas poke into logs and underground nests with their pointy snouts. Their long, sticky tongues lick up ants and termites. Aardvarks have piglike snouts to sniff out insects, and long, thin tongues to catch them. Moles cannot see well so they use their noses to find food.

An echidna can burrow underground in less than one minute.

An echidna

10

► An echidna's mouth is at the tip of its snout. It has no teeth and can open its mouth only wide enough to allow its tongue to go in and out.

tongue darts in and out

◄ Howler monkeys can roar loudly because they have huge voice boxes.

Heads and Tails

In the forests of Madagascar, an island off the coast of Africa, the cries of ring-tailed lemurs echo through the night. With faces like ghosts, and long tails that wave in the air, they look for fruits and insects. Ring-tailed lemurs live mainly on the ground, but other lemurs live in the trees. Howler monkeys swing through the trees in South American forests using their long tails. These monkeys have loud, howling roars. They can be heard up to three miles away!

Howler monkeys often swing by their tails while they eat.

▲ Ring-tailed lemurs
have unusual heads and
tails. They smear their
tails with their own scent
and wave them at enemies
during fights.

In the Trees

Many different kinds of monkeys live high in the trees. Cotton-top tamarins are some of the most colorful. They have long tails, squirrel-like faces, and silky white hair that flows down to their shoulders. Proboscis monkeys live in the forests of Borneo, and can swim in rivers. Gibbons look like monkeys, but they are actually related to apes. Like other apes, such as gorillas and chimpanzees, gibbons do not have tails. They swing along branches by placing one hand after the other on the branch.

▲ Gibbons have long fingers that hook onto branches. Their strong arms are twice as long as their bodies.

▲ Proboscis means "long snout." The nose of the male proboscis monkey grows much longer than the nose of the female.

Monkeys, apes, and humans all belong to a group called primates.

14

▲ Families of cotton-top
tamarins live together in
rainforest trees. They eat
fruits, leaves, and insects,
and make high-pitched
calls to each other.

15

◄ A squirrel glider does not have wings like a bat. It glides through the air using a special flap of skin that runs from the ankle to the wrist.

In the Air

Just before it gets dark at night, look up at the sky. You might see the black shapes of bats as they fly to their feeding grounds. At dawn, they return to their dark homes to hang upside down and sleep. Bats live everywhere in the world, except the cold lands of the Antarctic and Arctic. They are the only mammals that can fly. Some bats eat insects, while others eat fruit. The common vampire bat drinks the blood of large mammals and birds.

► Flying foxes are the largest bats of all. The gray-haired flying fox lives in Australia and can see well with its large eyes.

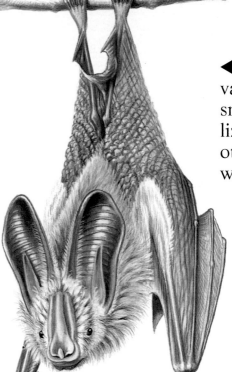

◀ The yellow-winged false vampire bat eats insects, small animals such as lizards and mice, and even other bats. It hears well with its large ears.

If a vampire bat drinks too much blood, it may be too full to fly.

▶ The common vampire bat cuts the skin of chickens, donkeys, or cattle with its razor-sharp front teeth. It laps up the blood with its tongue.

Under the Sea

▶ This is a male ribbon eel. Females are yellow with black fins. Ribbon eels weave their slimy bodies into small spaces.

The sea covers two-thirds of the Earth. The creatures that live within this hidden world seem very mysterious. Brightly colored fish shelter in coral reefs in warm, shallow seas. Giant squid, with eight waving arms and two tentacles, swim in deep waters. Ribbon eels slither into cracks and caves and wait for prey, which they seize with their jaws. The Pacific hagfish also has a long, eel-like body. With its sharp teeth it bores into dead fish and eats them from the inside out.

▶ Toadfish have slimy skin and bulging eyes, like toads, and are often brown and gray. But this toadfish, which lives in coral reefs, is the brightest in the family.

18

From the tip of their tentacles to the end of their bodies, giant squid can be as long as 66 feet.

▲ Giant squid are the largest animals without a backbone (invertebrates) in the world. Sperm whales like to eat them.

▶ Pacific hagfish can tie themselves into knots to wriggle out of an enemy's grasp.

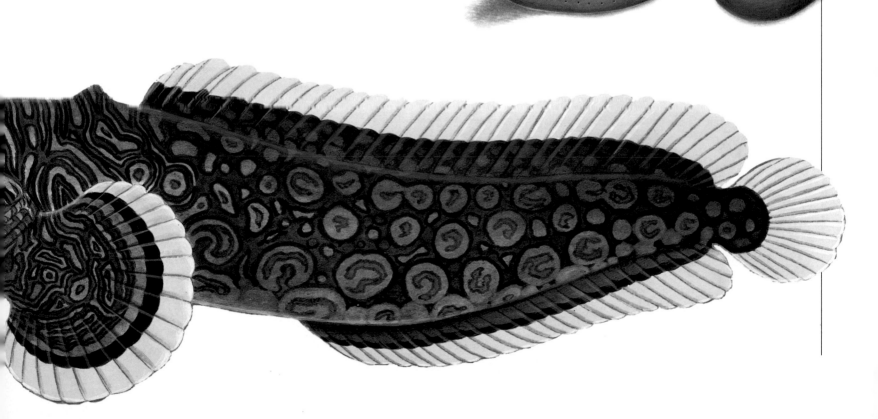

Armed for Life

Animals face many dangers. Some can run fast or burrow quickly into the ground to escape from predators. Others are protected by special body armor. The three-banded armadillo has hard plates of bone over its body. Tortoises and turtles have a bony shell as part of their skeleton. Many can pull their heads and legs inside their shells so that no part of them is uncovered. The spined, or cogwheel, turtle has dangerous-looking spines to keep attackers away.

▲ Only young spined, or cogwheel, turtles have these sharp spines on their shells.

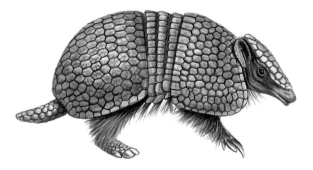

◀ The three-banded armadillo can fold its head and tail under its belly so that it forms a tight little ball.

20

▶ Giant saddleback tortoises have a raised part, like a saddle, in the front of their shells. This gives them room to stretch their necks to get food and water from cactus plants.

Armadillos come out at night. They often spend the day curled up tight.

Black rhinos puff like steam engines when they charge at their enemies.

◀ While a black rhino nibbles on a tree with its gripping upper lip, an oxpecker bird eats ticks and lice from the rhino's skin.

Rhinos

Rhinoceroses are heavy, lumbering animals. With fierce-looking horns, tough, leathery skin, and short, thick legs to hold up their bodies, they are some of the largest mammals living on land. Both the black rhino and the white rhino live in Africa. They are more of a gray color than black or white. Like all rhinos, they eat huge amounts of plants each day, and wallow in waterholes. A coating of mud on their skin helps to keep the flies away.

22

▲ White rhinos often form a circle to protect themselves and their calves.

▶ The white rhino is the biggest rhino of all, but it is easily frightened by people. It feeds on short grasses with its broad lips.

◀ When crested porcupines are threatened, they rattle their quills and stomp their feet. Then they try to stab their attacker with their quills.

A prickly skin

— INCREDIBLE CREATURES —

Prickly Creatures

Some creatures look very prickly. With horns, knobs, warts, and tough scales, the thorny devil of Australia suits its name perfectly. This lizard lives in dry places where there is little rain. But when there is morning dew, water collects between the lizard's bumps and runs along the grooves into its mouth. Porcupines have long, hollow spines called quills. The crested porcupine has its quills in the air all the time. But the quills of the tree porcupine stand up only when it is in danger.

How does a crested porcupine defend itself?

◀ The tree porcupine grips onto branches with its tail. It moves from tree to tree, looking for leaves to eat.

keeps attackers away

▲ The thorny devil looks much more fierce than it is. This strange lizard eats ants, and moves very slowly in the hot desert sun.

Searching for Prey

Goanna is the Australian name for a large monitor lizard.

▲ A European slow worm looks like a snake, but has eyelids, earholes, and a wider, shorter tongue.

▲ Goannas are powerful lizards. They eat eggs, mammals, and small lizards.

Animals catch prey in different ways. Some use dangerous horns, speed, or sharp teeth. Others have more unusual methods. The alligator snapping turtle opens its mouth wide and waves the pink, fleshy part on its tongue. When curious fish come close to see if they can eat it—SNAP! The turtle seizes them in its strong jaws. A European slow worm and a goanna flick out their forked tongues to pick up special scents from the ground or the air. These scents give them information about prey.

Sitting very still, jaws wide open

▼ The alligator snapping turtle is a big freshwater turtle with a small shell. Because it cannot hide in its shell, it uses its strong jaws to defend itself.

Looking at Lizards

▲ The sail-tailed lizard lies in the sun on rocks and branches near the water.

▼ The tail of a tree dragon is nearly four times as long as its body.

Lizards are all shapes, sizes, and colors. The shape of a lizard's body gives us clues about where and how it lives. Monitor lizards, the largest lizards of all, live on land and have strong, powerful bodies. They can run quickly for short distances. The tree dragon lizard has a long, narrow body for slithering along the branches of trees. The sail-tailed lizard spends some time in the water and has a special tail for swimming. The marine iguana is the only lizard that lives in the sea.

Sail-tailed lizards can run on water for a short way before they sink.

▶ Gould's goanna lives in Australia. When this monitor lizard is threatened or wants to get a better view of its surroundings, it raises itself up on its strong legs.

▲ The male marine iguana is usually dark gray or black. But when it breeds with females, it becomes a bright color like this.

Scorpions and Spiders

Scorpions and spiders scare many people. But most of these small, eight-legged creatures will not harm people. Scorpions have stinging tails and grasping pincers at the end of two of their legs. They grip insects, spiders, and other scorpions with these pincers, and then kill them with a sting from their tail. Spiders live all around the world. Some are tiny, but others can be as big as your hand. Spiders bite people to defend themselves. Only about 30 kinds of spiders have poison that can kill humans.

▲ A bite from the funnel-web spider of Australia can be fatal. It injects venom into its prey with the two large fangs at the front of its head.

▶ A female nursery-web spider sometimes eats the smaller male. To distract the female, the male gives her an insect wrapped in silk. While she is eating, he can mate with her safely.

▼ A scorpion's tail ends in a hook, which is the scorpion's stinger. Poison flows from the scorpion's stinger into its victim.

Scorpions can have between six and twelve eyes.

Other titles in the series:

ANIMAL BABIES
MIGHTY DINOSAURS
SCALY THINGS
THINGS WITH WINGS
UNDERWATER ANIMALS

Acknowledgments

(t=top, b=bottom, l=left, r=right, c=center, F=front cover,
B=back cover)

Simone End, 4tl, 10cl, 19tr, 29r. **Christer Eriksson,** 27c,
30tr, 31c. **John Francis/Bernard Thornton Artists, UK,** 21c,
24/25c. **David Kirshner,** Ftr, B, 2, 3br, 6tl, 6/7c, 8tl, 9tr,
12tl, 16tl, 16r, 17tl, 17br, 18l, 18/19bc, 19cr, 20tl, 20 bl,
22l, 23r, 23tl, 25tl, 28tl, 28bl, 29bl, 32. **John Mac/Folio,**
10tl, 10bl. **James McKinnon,** 1, 14bl, 14/15, 24tl.
Colin Newman/Bernard Thornton Artists, UK, 26cl, 26bl.
Barbara Rodanska, 30bc. **Peter Schouten,** 3tl, 4/5c, 5br,
12/13c, 14tr. **Kevin Stead,** Fb, 8/9c, 11.